I0559273

THE
LITTLE
BOOK
OF
SHORT
STORIES

DJ ROBBIE G

Copyright © 2023 by DJ Robbie G

Paperback: 978-1-963050-65-3
eBook: 978-1-963050-66-0
Library of Congress Control Number: 2023923792

All rights reserved. No part of this publication may be reproduced, distributed, or transmitted in any form or by any electronic or mechanical means, without the prior written permission of the publisher, except in the case of brief quotations embodied in critical reviews and certain other noncommercial uses permitted by copyright law.

This Book is a work of fiction. Names, characters, places, and incidents either are the product of the author's imagination or are used fictitiously. Any resemblance to actual persons, living or dead, events, or locales is entirely coincidental.

Ordering Information:

Prime Seven Media
518 Landmann St.
Tomah City, WI 54660

Printed in the United States of America

Table of Contents

The trip to the outhouse.

3 am, wind is howling outside, and branches are making noises up against the house, creating a horrible scratching sound. Particularly a squeaking sound against the windows, a tapping noise also can be heard.

Jeff, is slowly waking up due to the noises outside, he looks at the alarm clock, "are you serious, 4 hours still to go, sheesh" says Jeff with the annoyed attitude. He looks around the room to see the pet dog, Max, sitting up watching Jeff, as Jeff swings his legs around from under the covers and sits on the side of his bed.

Jeff looks over towards his wife Linda, she is very much asleep, very deep in sleep that she is snoring.

"Typical" says Jeff as he holds his face in his face, and rubbing his eyes.

He gets up and walks towards the door, Max follows, they walk through the hallway, to the bathroom, Jeff goes to open the door, the light is on and a little voice says "I'm in here" says his 5 year old daughter Maysie.

"OK honey, I go outside", says Jeff.

He and Max, go towards the lounge room, through the lounge to the dinning area, where they stop infront of a large glass sliding door to the backyard.

"Well Max, we have to venture out in the wind, are you game?" Max looks at Jeff, like come on let's go .

Then, heavy, saturating rain, falling outside, the type that will fill up your water tanks very quickly, or starts flash flooding, but even so, Jeff and Max, they need the toilet, and now, they need to venture out in wind, rain, thunder and lightning.

The sliding door opens, they step out, still slightly under cover, Jeff runs, on his tipping toes, to the outhouse, he reaches it, gets in,with a sigh of relief, he does his buisness, finishes, then goes out the door, runs on his tipsy toes back to the house, Max runs alongside Jeff, just before he reaches the house, he steps in Max's buisness, " oh man, are you serious" rain still belting down, over to the garden hose, grabs the hose, turns it on and washes his foot.

They get inside, totally wet, "all that just to go to the toilet, time to do some home renovations Maxy boy" Jeff says while rubbing Max over with a towel.

Jeff goes and has a shower and then back to bed.

Max gets back on his bed, but not fully asleep, always on guard, always aware of everything around him.

The End

The night out on the town, gone wrong!

*I*t's a beautiful spring day/night, and Tim has the night off work. Tim is a crowd controller and works at Stella's every Thursday, Friday and Saturday night. Tim is going in to where he normally works as its his birthday and a drink card has been arranged for Tim.

Tim shares a house with 4 other people, and they are all going with Tim for a few drinks for his birthday.

Tim is wearing jeans with a white short sleeve top, not really dressed to kill hearts just casual.

His house mates, Tracy, John,Patrick and Tina are all in the livingroom waiting for Tim to finish his getting ready routine.

"Come on Tim, they'll be closed soon" said John being sarcastic, "yeah right, gotta be right for the girls you know, can't dissapoint them" Tim replied, he was smiling at himself at the mirror, playing with his hair. Tim had short back and sides haircut, he was an ex soldier in the Royal Australian Army. He was fit, he would frequently visit the gym to keep bulking up the muscle.

"OK Tim taxis is here" Tina yelled

"Let's go" Tim yells as he goes out the door first, " come on, ive been waiting for all you guys to get ready all night, they'll be closed soon" smiled Tim as he got in the taxis. "You cheeky little bugger" said Patrick. They all got in the Taxis, and headed off to Stella's.

The Taxis trip to Stella's was a great trip, singing, joking, lots of laughing, happy bday being sung over and over.

They arrive at Stella's, and they all get out and head toward the from entrance of the club. The music can be heard thumping through the door as it opens and shuts.

"Happy birthday Tim" Brian who is the manager, hands Tim an envelope, Tim opens it and it's a birthday card, and he finds a $150 drink card inside. "Woah thanks mate" Tim shakes Brian's hand, "off ya go buddy, go have some fun", off they go inside the club as a tight knit group.

They get to the bar, Tracy and Tina get their drinks, then leave them with John and Patrick at they bar. They go off to hit the dance floor.

Tim, John and Patrick are sitting at the end of the bar, but its a quiet comfortable little spot with no one to annoy them.

John and Patrick get on the scotch and cokes, time is getting on the midori shakes, and he is guzzling them down.

Shots, shakes drinks partying all through the night, 5 hours later, and Tim has seen better days.

He felt a pain in the stomach, like maybe he needed to go sit on the toilet kind of pain.

He got off the bar stool, and nearly fell down on the floor, due to sitting and drinking the whole time.

So he starts walking, well more like staggering towards the bathroom, he found it hard to tell which was the men's and which was the ladies toilets, as it was Gay night at Stella's, guys in drag, lesbians in drag, everything happening, he finds the men's toilet, staggers to the cubicle, pants down, sits down, waits a little bit, burping, the all of a sudden, Tim power chucks, straight down into his pants, and it goes on for about 2 minutes.

No carrots, no food just the 15 midori shakes and different shots he had.

"Oh yeah, happy bday to me, are you kidding me, how the? What the? Why?"

For the next hour, Tim stayed in the cubicle to clean up his pants, made it easier that there was no food in the chunder, the hard part was having to put the pants back on.

He had to get them back on as so he could leave to get home.

"Ergh oh my, oh yuck, why me" Tim in disgust, got the pants back on, but in protest of doing it. He now goes to find his friends, but finds, the club has emptied, 10 minutes to closing, Brian walks up, "oh my mate, what did you do, your friends have gone home. Did you pee yourself, my God mate you're a mess!"

Out the door of Stella's, and gets into the taxis, sits down very uncomfortably due to wet pants, not the most comfortable feeling.

Taxi driver says, " Do not throw up in my cab"!

Tim needs to throw up, while the taxi is still driving, slowly, holding onto the door, throwing up at the same time. This happens 3 times, till he gets home, he pays the Taxi driver. Looks at his watch, 4:57am.

"Happy birthday Tim " then feels his wet pants, "yep, not doing that again" .

Tim goes inside, shuts the door, goes to his room, strip's off, showers and bed.

Oh what a night!

Bad 1st day.

*I*t's a very hot day in the middle of October, and Jim has just met the criteria to join the Royal Australian Army.

He is on the bus travelling from Melbourne to Wagga Wagga, where he will be spending 13 weeks at Kapooka known as 1 Recruit Training Battalion.

The corporal's on the bus, are being very nice, talking very nicely to all, approximately 48 to 52 young men about to become soldiers.

They are sharing stories, funny ones, telling funny jokes, being very friendly with all the men like they were best friends for years.

Some men were quiet, and anxious, wondering and pondering if they had made the right decision to join.

The bus came to a stop at a roadhouse, which was a scheduled halfway stop to have lunch, and the corporal's were very polite, guiding all to where they had to go, where the menu was, everyone felt at ease like they were meant to be there, even the ones full of anxiety and unease were not too worried.

30 minutes went by and everyone was to get back on the bus as a schedule had to be kept. The corporal's were fantastic, they made

everyone feel good about themselves, no one had a worry in the world. Jim was pondering about a few things like how long did he want to stay in the Army, when was he going to see his Mum and Dad and brothers and sisters again. Does he get to go home for Christmas? Questions, questions questions he thought.

30 minutes away from getting to Kapooka, one of the corporal's got up, and said very loudly and sternly, "okay, we are 30 minutes away from your destination, where it will make you, or break you, 30% of you will drop out, I suggest you sit in silence, and contemplate your 13 weeks, coz it's starts now.

Dead silence, its like the corporal had just lost an argument and just decided to take it out on others.

But that was nothing.

The bus arrived through the gates of kapooka, all 3 corporal's stood in the middle of the bus, all yelling, all screaming, swearing, calling individuals names, terrible names. The 3 corporal's were acting like they were having a bi polar episode.

Woah, what the? Jim was sitting there mouth wide open, looking at the other guy in the seat across from himself, to his surprise had the same reaction to what was going on.

The bus comes to a full stop, by this stage, its pouring down rain, and everyone rushes around in a panic, all had to stand in 3 straight lines, but because the corporal's were yelling and screaming, no one was able to think straight, and panic was setting into the men.

All had to do push ups, "lower" "raise" "lower".

Rain still bucketing down, everyone's luggage, getting wet, yelling and screaming still happening.

All recruits then marched towards the barracks they were to be roomed up, 4 to a room, you had 3 roomates that you had never met never spoken before, but you were to become great mates, looking out for eachother.

After hours of abuse and yelling, everyone was to get into bed, lights out at 10pm, just then, you could hear 4 maybe 5 men crying to themselves, obviously the shock of the introduction of the 1st day was too much.

Jim laid in bed, starring at the ceiling, thinking "WOW, what a 1st day, what have i got myself into", after a while of listening to the crying and sniffling he drifted off to sleep.

5:55am, the wake up call that no one should ever be woken up to if you have a bad heart.

The loud resounding, ear piercing, shock to the system sound of a M60 firing down the haway of the barracks. Firing blanks of course. Everyone to stand up straight to attention in the hallway, corporal's yelling, swearing, abuse abuse abuse. Jim standing there thinking,"this is it, 13 weeks of he'll, make ya or break ya. We'll, looks like your gonna make me"

The rude awakening

School holidays, what a great time it is for Tommy as he was getting ready to go stay on his Grand parents farm. Tommy loves his Grandparents and also idolises his Uncle Terry, Terry plays football in the local towns football club in Australian Rules Football. Tommy wants to grow up to be like his Uncle Terry.

Football is a huge phenomenon in the district, kids live to be like their fathers, uncles, grandfathers, or their hero's that play in the National AFL competition.

Tommy only 9, lives and dreams of being a top AFL player, he plays in the under 10's competition. He hasn't yet become what he would like to be, be he is trying hard.

Tommy's mum organises the car to take Tommy to the farm. The football had to go too coz whenever there was a chance, Tommy would hound his uncle to go have a kick of the footy.

Australian rules football is a very hard physical game of speed and stamina.

It's nothing like American Football, wearing helmets and padding, nothing like rugby, or soccer, it is a very complex game, you either have got it, or you don't.

Mum and Tommy get in the car and head out to the farm, on the way out to the farm mum stops at the petrol station to put fuel in the car, and she buys Tommy a drink, and then off they go.

Driving down the highway, Tommy is watching the huge gum trees going past as they drive past them. They are huge gum trees on both sides of the road.

Over the railway line and turns onto the dirt road leading to the farm.

Tommy's getting ants and excited, he can't wait to see his Grandparents, and also uncle Terry.

The car pulls up near the back gate is, and grandma's at the gate waving to Tommy, and he couldn't get out of the car quick enough. He trips over his feet to get over to his grandma, she laughs as he picks himself up, and then into her arms with a long long embrace.

Grandpa is coming over from the shed, he was working on getting the tractor ready for work tomorrow. Tommy was going to be with his grandpa on the tractor for the day, and he loves spending time with his grandfather.

Uncle Terry appeared from the shed as well, and he told his Dad the tractor was ready for work for the next day, then Tommy grabs his footy, and kicks it to Terry and then this goes on for about an hour, kicking it to eachother, over and over.

Then they get called into have dinner, Terry goes out to milk and feed the cows, Terry is 22 and has a girlfriend, after he finishes, he heads off to go visit his girlfriend.

Tommy has a bath, and gets all cleaned up, then it's off to bed, bedtime is 7:30 for Tommy, he doesn't like it, but he does what he is told.

Tommy is thinking about what tomorrow will bring, grandpa's stories always keeps Tommy enlightened, he loves his stories.

5 hours later, approximately 1am, Terry gets home from seeing his girlfriend, and the house is in darkness, he turns on the kitchen light, gets a drink of water, leaves the kitchen light on, then quietly goes into the his bedroom, Tommy is asleep on the bed across from Terry's bed.

Terry is in a bit of a funny mood, and laughs to himself.

"Tommy, Tommy," Terry whispers to Tommy and taps him on the shoulder.

Tommy rolls over, "Grandpa is waiting for you, you better get going"

Tommy gets up, gets dressed, goes out to the kitchen, lights on but no grandpa. Looks at the clock, "what" he storms back to the bedroom, "rude Uncle Terry "

Very rude indeed.

A Tiny Accident

*I*t's a beautiful summers night, and 5 year old Jack is sitting on the floor watching TV while his mum is cleaning up after dinner. She is a single mum and she has been dating a guy that works as a mechanic in the town.

His name is Ivan and he has been dating Sally for the last 6 months. Jack has been very protective of his mum. Whenever Sally and Ivan have gone out for dinner at the local pub, Jack becomes a bit of a handful, and gets into alot of trouble. For instance, one night for example, they were out for dinner at the local pub, and Jack wouldn't sit still. He was running around, bumping people, kicking chairs, punching and kicking people playing pool, running behind the bar and smashing glasses. Being a real Denise the menace. His behaviour can be an issue, and very embarrassing.

Sally and Ivan are in the kitchen cleaning up, and chatting about their day and what they had done, what issues they had to deal with.

Ivan had brought over a block of chocolate to sort of celebrate 6 months together. "For later tonight sweetness" Ivan held the block in the air. " Oh hell yeah, very much so" replied Sally.

"Jack, time for bed buddy" Sally yells out to Jack.

"OK mummy " says Jack as he comes running in and hugs his mother. Then bounces over to Ivan and jumps into his arms.

Ivan is the only male figure in Jack's life, and yet that still hasn't stopped Jack from being so protective and hanging around his mother like a bad smell.

Ivan takes Jack to bed, and reads him a story, and reads the wholes book to him, which takes about 15 minutes.

Then they talk about footy, animals,going to the playground over the weekend, ice cream tomorrow, soft drink tomorrow etc.

"Good night big fella" Ivan says to Jack giving him a hug. " Ivan, can I call you Daddy, other kids at kinder, well they all have a Daddy, and I want you to be my Daddy, please, pleeeeeeeeese" Jack being such a beautiful cute kid.

This is a question Ivan wasn't expecting, but had a feeling it would happen at some stage.

"Let's have a sleep on it mate, and we will talk to mummy tomorrow about it, ok " says Ivan with a big smile, "ok" and the fist bump.

"Goodnight mate" goodnight Jacky boy.

"goodnight" replies Jack.

3 hours later.

Jack has a habit of not going to sleep straight away and takes a good two hours for him to fall asleep, but he is wide awake tonight. He knows about the chocolate that his mum and Ivan are about to have.

Sally and Ivan go into check that Jack is asleep. The see Jack in bed eyes closed, asleep, they leave the room, Jack's eyes open, he then

THE LITTLE BOOK OF SHORT STORIES

gets out of bed, Ivan has gone to the outhouse, Sally in the inside bathroom.

Jack quietly goes into his mums bedroom, climbs into the wardrobe, with a slight gap, so he could see.

30 minutes later, Sally and Ivan go in and lay on the bed and start eating the chocolate together.

They talk about the future plans, and about Jack calling Ivan dad.

Just then, they could smell an off smell, like number 2's was near, then the slight sound of snoring, coming from the wardrobe.

Sally opens up the wardrobe, to find Jack totally asleep, and had soiled her slippers.

"Oh dear"

Bad night at work!

Springtime, a special smell in the air, there is no other smell like it, like grass freshly cut, leaves regrowing on the trees, a slight breeze in the air, and gives you a feeling of happyness.

Jason has woken up, he works as a crowd controller/bartender, starts at 7pm and finishes at 7am. The place he works at is a 24hr bar/club, and is very very rough.

Jason is fresh out of the military, trained with special skills. He was hired to try clean up the bar/club as it has been getting a reputation, in which if that starts, you lose your clients.

Jason has just had himself a shower, and getting ready for work, he has to walk to the tram stop, tram takes 20 minutes, and stops right in front of the bar/club. He likes to get there an hour early just in case he has to get anything done.

He arrives, and he has a quick walk around, not many people in at the moment, but its only early.

Time goes by, and there is now about 60 people in the bar/club, 3 other security/crowd controllers have turned up to work, which is a good thing, music has started and people are on the dance floor.

2 hours go by, and there is close to 100 people in the bar/club now, and trouble has started at the pool table. An argument has started, all over whose turn it was or wasn't.

Jason is onto it straight away, talks to them, restarts the game, and then all was fine. Then from out of nowhere, an eruption and boilover of anger and fighting starts at the pool table.

The security at the front door come in, they separate the fighting men, and start walking the men out to the front door.

Then, to everyone's surprise, one of the men produce a knife, and stabs one of the security, pulling his head down and stbbing him in the back, the other security try's to disarm the man with the knife, and they walk out onto the road, and the man stabs the security in the chest. Jason sees this all happening and quickly jumps the bar, goes through the bottles hop, 3 girls were standing, watching it all happen, Jason pushes them inside to protect them from the man with the knife.

While he was doing this, he felt pain hitting him in his back, neck, side, and arm. He turned around and the man with the knife, starring at him, then he turned and ran off.

Jason went to run off after him too, got down the road, and a police car pulled up beside him.

"get in"

They sped off in pursuit, but to no avail. Jason then felt a wetness on his left side. The police turned on the light inside the car. A huge patch of blood on the back seat, and it turned out, Jason had been stabbed 5 times.

Very bad night!

The big 40th.

avid wakes up to the Sunshine peeping through the curtains, straight into the eyeballs, not nice to wake up too. His wife Alice comes in with a coffee,

"Happy birthday honey, are you feeling older?, the big 40" Alice says to David as she puts his coffee on his side table.

David for the last 6 months had been working Friday nights to pay for his 40th party, the venue, the band, the alcohol, the food, the chocolate fountain, the photographer, etc.

Lots of planning, and alot of talk up and around all his friends and family.

David and Alice spent half the night setting up the venue the night before the big night.

They had photo's on the wall, white table cloths, with old style records on the tables. They had black lights on, so anything white luminates, and hanging records from the ceiling, and cds and old style cassette tapes.

There also was a giant banner made up for David's party, 2 babies, one laughing, the other crying, its a great picture, 3 metres by 1.5 meters. It's huge, and it's for everyone to sign and write something.

David has invited about 120 friends and family to come and celebrate his 40th with him.

David picks up his coffee, has a drink, Alice opens up the curtains, "ouch pre warning honey" as he covers up his eyes. "Well, not all of us are vampire's dear, its 10:30 and I have things to do if I'm to be at your party tonight," Alice explains, as she starts cleaning up the house. " and if the after party is happening after the main party, then you better get a move on too" says Alice while picking up dirty clothes.

"yes dear" replies David, ready for sleep again. He isn't a morning person at all. But tonight has him ready to push on through the tiredness.

They have a back shed 9metres by 9 metres, and it's a mancave, it resemble a night club, a huge bar build from work pallets, with enough alcohol to start up a bar in town .

Beer keg seats, lounge suite, 55 inch screen, hats, bottles, a reindeer, flags, posters and everything you can think of is hanging from the roof.

An outdoor fire built with beer kegs and more seats, BBQ and spit rotisserie. David had built a seating area out of treated pine with a table to rest your drinks or food, it was built to provide shelter if or when it rained so the party could keep going. It was built so the water would run off and not just sit on the roof. Every now and then when they would have people over, David would go to the bar fridge, grab a bottle of water, ice cold it would be, and if someone was standing at the right spot at the end of the shelter, David would reach up and pour the ice cold water on the roof, and because of the angle, it would run down and fall onto the person underneath.

David has a sense of humour. If your at his bbq and the fire is going, and you aren't paying attention, David can give you the fright of a lifetime. He does it every now and then, drops a log into the fire with a deoderant can and you won't notice. 1 or 2 minutes later, kaboom, the deodorant can explodes, it gives you a fright if you aren't expecting it.

David gets the after party all ready for the continuation of the night. Everything is all done and organised, beers and mixed drinks all on ice, fridge is full, music ready for background music.

House is all clean and presentable for the after party.

The party starts!

7:30pm starts and David and Alice are at the venue. It's a beautiful venue with a great title, "Ebony's ". They are great friend with the owners and David works behind the bar 5 nights a week.

People start coming through the door, and it's getting busy, everyone that was invited that weren't working, turned up, out of 120 invites 79 people show up.

The band start playing songs that David had requested them to do, and immediately the dance floor is full.

David has requested Aussie pub rock songs, songs he grew up with as a teenager, through the 80's .

David is drinking like a fish, he starts on beer, then later on during the night he went onto Jim Beam and coke. Jelly shots were also available, and David was getting very merry.

The birthday cake and speeches, well, it was the type of speeches that you couldn't afford to miss. They were memorable and hard to forget. David's speech was very hard to understand due to being very drunk, but repeatedly saying he loved his wife, he accidentally called her Allen in his speech and was told off by Alice at that time.

But everyone laughed and was very funny.

The night at "Ebony's" finished, and the after party was about to start. About 40 people went back to David and Alice's, the background music wasn't very loud as they had neighbours, some were there, but still be mindful of other neighbours.

Surprisingly, after everyone has left, David is last man standing, he sits there at his bar in the shed, beer in hand, raises his beer in the air, "Thankyou God for the privilege of being alive, I love you".

From hell to salvation!

*E*veryone has a story, everyone goes through terrible things, life is a journey, live everyday like it's your last day on earth!

This story starts way before Jamie was born. Jamie's mother Mary was dating Peter, and it was a very toxic violent relationship.

Peter was a mechanic, and his family migrated from Germany when he was 8. Peter and Mary had been dating for 2 years now, and Mary had just found out she was pregnant. Mary was happy, but also worried about how Peter would react.

Mary's thoughts were right, Peter went off his head, he became so violent that he thrashed Mary around, braking her nose, kicked her repeatedly in the stomach, trying to get her to lose the baby.

This behaviour continued all through the pregnancy, then Mary gave birth, to a beautiful boy, Jamie, but he was crying all the time, he was a stressed baby, but let's face it, with all the violence that Mary had gone through, it would have stressed out baby Jamie in the womb.

The stress was intense, and the violence would occur daily, physically, and mentally, it was draining, and Mary was near breaking point.

Peter ended up getting arrested for stealing, and beating up some guys in a bar, he produced a gun, and he ended up in jail for 12 months.

But still, for some ridiculous reason, Mary stuck by Peter, she would visit him in jail every Friday, right through the whole 12 months. When Peter got out of jail, he went to the bar, he drank, got drunk, went home, broke up the house inside, picked up 14 month old Jamie by the foot, threw him into the wall because he was crying. Mary was screaming and finally standing up to Peter, she hit him with a golf club, cracked him a good one. She then picked up Jamie, he was very distraught, but there was no apparent injuries to little Jamie.

Police were called, and Peter was arrested again.

Mary needed out, she needed to do whatever it took, to keep her baby boy safe.

She and Jamie were now safe, they had moved to Mary's parents farm, and Peter was to be in jail for 2 years for what he had done. You would think that he would have been given more than 2 years.

Through the court order, Peter was not to be within 100ft, of Mary and Jamie, to not have contact with Jamie untill he turns 15 years old.

14 years later!

On Jamie's 15th birthday, they were having his birthday party at the farm. The phone rings, and it's Peter, Jamie's father. He knows only a small amount of things about his father, Mary wasn't that sort of mother, but her and Jamie were at loggerheads with eachother, all Jamie wants is to know and feel he is loved. He has been difficult to deal with, the older he gets the worse his anxiety becomes, and now, he has to deal with someone he doesn't know at all, his father!

Mary keeps an eye on Jamie, to make sure he doesn't get too stressed. The conversations finishes, and it's organised to have Jamie stay for a week during holidays.

Mary hates this idea, but has to go along with it.

Tension and anger builds between Mary and Jamie, it shouldn't be like this at all, but Mary has good reason to be upset. She has protected her son from a monster, and now her son is willingly walking into the arms of evil.

During the holidays, before Jamie goes to his father's house, Mary hugs her son, holds him very tight, "I'm only a phone call away"

"OK mum"

Jamie arrives at his father's house and meets his father's wife and their kids. Theresa is peters wife, she is 10 years older than Peter, Leanne, Kelly and Cameron are the kids they have together.

For the whole week went nicely, got along well with the kids, with Theresa, and also with his father.

It was offered that he came to live with them the start of the next year. When Jamie got home, he shared with his mother what was about to happen.

Mary was gutted, and for the next 6 weeks refused to talk to Jamie.

For a 15 year old, it hurt him, he knew his mother was upset, but why not talk to him. It showed him she didn't love him, that was pushing him away.

He decided that he was moving earlier than the next year, it was next week.

Mary still wouldn't talk to him, nothing was going to change the situation, Jamie was desperate for a change, he hated the atmosphere at home, and needed change.

The day came where Jamie was to move to his father's house, where he felt wanted, he wanted to be loved. Jamie was confident that he was making the right choice.

So he thought!

After living at his father's house, his father Peter started showing his violent side. And Jamie copped his 1st broken nose. He had left a light on, and his father had been drinking. Jamie lived there for 7 months, during that 7 months he had his nose broken 7 times, ribs broken wrist broken head smashed with a metal star picket, then the worst of the worst, pushed into a cupboard and petrol poured all over and in and over him. His father threatened to light him up. The stress that Jamie had gone through the whole entire time was absolutely horrible.

No human being should ever go through anything like that ever.

Jamie decided to leave the next day, his father goes to work early, his step mum leaves early for work, he was going to hitch-hike and get away back to his mother's.

Morning came, instead of going to school, he got on his bike, road as far as he was able down the highway, Jamie had ridden about 20 kilometres down the highway. He decided to hitch-hike now, he was exhausted.

So out came the thumb, and straight up, an old Ford F1100 truck pulls up, the driver a very ugly old man with an eye patch, "where are you headed young man" he asked

"I'm going to Ballarat, I'm going to my Aunty's" Jamie replied as he gets in the truck. Jamie looks at all the quotes on the dashboard, they were all bible scriptures, one quote stood out more than the scriptures .

It wasn't a scripture, just a quote, "the person operating this vehicle, may disappear at any time".

Huh, what the? Thought Jamie to himself.

The trip comes to an end, and the man has to wake up Jamie to let him know he is at his Aunty's house.

The funny thing is how did the man know where his Aunty lived, who was this man.

Jamie went and knocked on the door of his Aunty's house, his Aunty answered, Jamie was pretty much very un recognisable with all the bruises over his face.

"Jamie?" his Aunty says stunned to see Jamie, " how did you get here?"

"The man in the truck" Jamie turned around, but the man in the truck was gone. Didn't even hear the truck go.

3 hours later Mary turned up to pick up Jamie, there was a great emotional healing between mother and son.

Mary drove Jamie home, it was a long 3 hour trip home, and as soon as they arrive home, they hit their beds and get some sleep. The next day Mary takes Jamie to the police station to report everything to the police, he was asked if he wanted to lay charges,

"No, that means he will see me, he doesn't deserve that right" Jamie replied.

2 months later, Jamie was invited to a pentecostal church, he wasn't too sure whether to go or not, but he went, and the experience of walking into a huge welcome, it was like he was home, and the love he had been chasing was here.

There was beautiful music, the preaching was on target with a great message, 'He leaves the 99 to go after the 1' the message really hit Jamie, and the call came for those that wanted to give their heart to Jesus the Saviour, and Jamie ran to the alter, he was crying, uncontrollable crying.

He gave his heart to Jesus!

He is saved!

Misplaced keys to the car!

*I*t's a glorious sunny morning, and Matthew has just woken up. The time is 11am and Matthew doesn't have a job. He stays up untill 3 or 4 in the morning, and has been in that routine for approximately 12 months now. He has no confidence to hold down a job, and he had a accident at work.

He was working in a timber mill, he had fallen from a height of 2 metres and broken his shoulder (humouress) bone, and also had ruptured the acl and rotator cuff.

It wasn't just the injury that caused issues with confidence, he also suffers from severe depression and severe anxiety. His routine on a daily basis was interrupted due to the accident causing injury.

He is living alone, which makes it so much harder, no one around to bounce off conversation with. He has a doctors appointment in an hour, and is all ready to go attend.

He normally has the keys hanging on a hook in the kitchen, but they aren't there. He goes to his bedroom, searches through his bedside draws, his clothes from yesterday, his jacket?

Then the bathroom, trying to remember where he had them last. Back in the bedroom, searching everywhere 4 times over. Then the loungeroom, over and over again.

He thought, maybe the shed, so out there he walks, getting anxious, and angry, goes in the shed, and goes through the whole shed, he has made the place look untidy trying to find the keys.

He walks past the car and out of the corner of his eye, he notices the windows half down, and unlocked.? What the?

He walks over and opens the driver's side door, and there, sitting in the ignition, the keys!

Why would you?

The wedding.

A beautiful spring day, the 23rd of September, and today is the day that Paul and Kelly are to be married.

Kelly has 4 girls all under 7, they are 7, 5, 3 and 1. Paul has 2 kids to a previous marriage, they are boy 13, and girl 11.

Paul and Kelly were briefly dating for about 4 months before getting engaged, they knew what they wanted, Paul wanted to fulfil Kelly's life, and show her love and affection, and also he was taking on her girls as his own.

Today has been planned to perfection. Paul stayed at the local pastors house the night before. The weekend before he went out for his bux party.

It wasn't a big thing, spent the night at his best friends house having coffee and biscuits.

Jim was Paul's best friend. He was also Paul's best man and they met a few years ago singing karaoke at The Key nightclub. It was organised the best man and the groom arrive at the wedding on Harley Davidson motorbikes.

Kelly was to arrive in a black limousine with her Dad and 4 daughters.

So the big day, it's getting real, 9:30 am and Paul has just woken up. He is very nervous, but very calm, the wedding ceremony was to happen at 2 pm, and Paul has nothing else to do, as everything is already organised.

Kelly has been up since 6:30 am with the make-up lady there, and also the hairdresser, and photographer, also her mum and her dad.

Her brother turns up with his 4 year old Son because because he is the ring bearer.

The photographer takes alot of pictures of Kelly getting ready, also of the girls too.

It gets to 12 midday and Paul gets a phone call about an old lady at the park where the ceremony was to happen, she was starting up the BBQ, and pulling down the flowers, Paul was angry, but was told to stay where he was, and to Paul's protest, he stayed. The florist had deterred the old lady, and she disappeared. The florist fixed up the flowers, and cleaned up the BBQ.

Everything was ready.

1:30pm, and Paul and his best man are out the front waiting for the Harley's, and they turn up, the are the most beautiful sounding machine coming from down the road.

The both get on the back of the Harley's, then the two Harley's head down the road, they are loud and proud, they go down the main street, the go back through the main street to go back to where the ceremony is about to happen.

Approximately 70-80 people were at the park, and it's a beautiful sunny day. Paul is saying hi to everyone that we're waiting as he moves to where his life is about to change for the better.

2:05pm and the black limousine arrives, tears roll down Paul's face as he sees the girls all dressed up in their beautiful dresses, and the little ring bearer, dressed in a cute little suit, and then, his future wife to be.

She is a picture of absolute beauty, and Paul is really getting excited, he feels like yelling and screaming because he is so excited.

They arrive, and the pastor starts with all the formalities, and then it came to the rings, and that's when disaster hits. Kelly's ring had been pulled off the cushion, Paul's was still there, but Kelly's was gone.

This started panic, but straight away, Kelly's mum stepped up and put her ring on the cushion to help the wedding proceed.

All the I do's, were done and dusted, it shows you a big lesson, where there is love, no matter what bad things happen, stay focused, let Gods love Guide you!

What God has brought together, let no man separate.

Throwing rocks causes pain.

A cold winters day and Steve is at the football. It's a home game, and Steve is allowed out of the car to go play with other friends.

Steve is 9 years old and has some behaviour issues at home also at school, and anywhere else he happens to be.

So he ventures over about 100 metres away from where the game is being played, and their are about 12 other kids Steve's age hanging around piles of dirt all in a long line.

The piles of dirt were going to be turned into a bitumen road for firemen to do fire drills.

There really wasn't much to do for kids in a small town, but when they did get together to do things, it usually ended up in trouble. Especially for little Steve. Trouble seemed to follow Steve wherever he went.

Steve had ADHD and anxiety, mental illness, but he was trying to not get into trouble, he just thought differently to the other kids, which was frustrating.

All the kids started to throw stones at the bin, at the fence, the shed roof etc.

Until they all decided to split up and be about 30 meters from eachother and start bombarding eachother.

Just as expected, Steve's Stone found the side of one of the kids head, hit her right in the temple area, a bad spot to be hit.

All the kids tendered to the girl, Steve ran over and seen all the blood. Steve's heart was pounding very fast, and then ran off to home, he was frightened, and very scared. He had hurt someone, he didn't mean to but he did.

His mother asked him why he wasn't at the footy, but Steve stayed in his room, scared, and after a couple of hours, knock at the door!

The father of the kid the stone had hit was at the door. He spoke to Steve's step-dad, then his step-dad looked at Steve. Steve's face had gone so red it was like a traffic light.

His Step-Dad was very upset, he was a very upstanding man and fully respected in the town, people look up to him. He drove Steve to the injured child's house, and knocked on the door. The kid and his dad were at the door, the kid had received 10 stitches because of impact of the stone that Steve had thrown.

Steve was very embarrassed and said he was sorry. This was the first time Steve was to experience forgiveness. The thing is, Steve didn't realise that where he hit the other kid, it could of killed him. The temple on the head is a dangerous place to be hit.

But the only way to move forward is to forgive!

The raspberry Creek dance.

*I*t's muggy and humid, wet and muddy, rain is pouring down, it's like buckets of water being thrown down from the clouds. It's 2 in the afternoon,, and the Army is on manouvers. They have been driving for almost 16 hours, and have arrived at the place on the map which was just before the road turnoff to Dawin to play war games.

Graeme had been in the service as a cook in his unit for nearly 3 years. Ha was with another cook with the unit . Their unit had 560 men and women, the unit was an aviation unit, they flew porter planes, helicopters eg blackhawks, snookes etc.

Every now and then Graeme recieved the chance to have a joy flight.

When on exercise, you end up doing everything you would do if in a war situation. This includes guard duty at night time. Graeme was put on guard duty for the first night, at midnight for 2 hours. Even though he was cooking for his unit, guard duty still had to be done.

The unit kitchen was set up, and first official meal served up and it was a success. Even though it is raining, it's very hot and very humid. It the wet season where they, 250 kms away from Darwin.

Everything is all cleaned up and Graeme decides he will get some sleep before his turn doing guard duty.

Straight away he is asleep, the 16 hours in the Army truck has tottally wrecked him. 11:40 pm and he is woken up by his foot being tapped to wake up.

Graeme grabs his water proof atire, and his rifle, and webbing and pack, walks slowly and quietly to where he has to sit in a trench for guard duty. There is another soldier on guard with Graeme, he is new to the unit, he is a nice person and everyone seems to like him.

An hour goes by and no sign of anything or anyone or any movement at all. Graeme looks over and sees the other guy on guard duty asleep. So he taps him on the shoulder very gently and all of a sudden his rifle fires off a shot, his rifle wasn't on safety. In these war games only blanks are used, but even that being the case, this was a major issue. Everyone was woken up by the shot, and the sergent had to report the issue to the commanding officer the next day.

It was unfortunate but the guy was charged, and fined $500, it was a sad day for him. But you learn from your mistakes. It was midday when the sergent came around asking if anyone was interested in going out on the Saturday night, it was the traditional raspberry creek. The Jeep was to pick up those going at 6:30 pm, to be dressed in neat and tidy civilian clothes and to be respectful of the ladies.

When out bush with the Army, you find ways to have fun, this was one.

Saturday came very quickly and there was 8 young bloke's, dressed neat and tidy. Nice clothing, they all jumped in the back of the Jeep which was covered over and they couldn't see out.

They were then driven around the camp sites which was fairly large area, and driven over some very bumpy terrain, this went on for about 30 minutes, then the Jeep backed up to a small creek, with waist high water, then ordered by the sergent to get out quickly.

All of them in their excitement, fell into the water. Everyone laughed themselves silly. The good old raspberry creek dance.

The life changing incidents.

*I*t's a thursday and in the middle of the day, Ben is organising the weekend of work functions, he is a karaoke /DJ host, and works in the country pub in a town called Morwell.

He has a big weekend of work coming up, a Friday night of karaoke at a friend's house, then Saturday night he has a private function in the back room of the venue he works at, and also a karaoke Grand Final in the front bar. It was all under control with someone doing the Grand Final while Ben does the private function.

What hasn't been told to Ben is that the pub couldn't get security for the private function.

This is the 1st incident.

Ben finds out on the Saturday about the issue with security. Ben then finds out he isn't doing the private function, the manager organised for the clients to use a i-pod for their music entertainment. Which means Ben loses $450 for that night of work.

Then Ben calls up the person that was doing the karaoke grand final, he cancels them as Ben needs to work to put food on the table and pay some bills.

While Ben is setting up his equipment for the grand final, the manager walks over to Ben, and tells Ben that he got a call from the other DJ complaining he wasn't working the grand final.

Let's face it, $450 is alot of money. The manager said he wants the other dj to do the night. So Ben says it's his buisness and he is not letting anyone tell him who or when someone will work for him. If they wanted the other dj, then they aren't using his equipment. So he started packing his equipment up.

This is the 2nd incident.

The manager comes over again, knowing Ben is packing his stuff up, he hands him a receipt, for 2 years worth of dinner meals that were meant to be part of the work agreement.

Ben has all his equipment out from the front bar, and tells them he will be back during the week to get all the equipment out of the nightclub area.

Ben has alot of sound and lighting equipment, over $40,000 worth. But the manager said to p- off and don't come back.

This is the 3rd incident.

Ben gets a phonecall that he is wanted to do a disco, short notice, but its money Ben needs. Bills are building up, which brings alot of pressure. So he takes along his 10 year old daughter, as the party is at a friend's house, they set up and it's pouring down rain, but the gear is safe and dry in the huge shed where the party is happening.

After setting up, Ben has an hour spare, so he gets in the car with his daughter and heads home to change.

It's really pouring down, very heavy rain. He is at the lights in front of Kentucky Fried Chicken, Ben is waiting for the lights to turn green. Then out from nowhere, a huge collision from behind, it collides twice.

Ben's daughter is absolutely scared and is screaming.

Ben's chair in the car has come out of the floor, his knees collapsed under the dashboard, a terrible pain in his lower back, is extremely painful. Both shoulders are feeling like they were hyper extended.

Ben in shock calms his daughter down, and makes sure she isnt hurt, then gets out of the car, to check on the other driver.

Ben gets to the other car, and the girl driving was very young.

She only wanted to find her phone, because she was on the phone.

This angered Ben but he kept his cool as it wasn't going to be a good look telling her off.

Police were notified, and they didn't turn up as they were way to busy to attend.

After a while Ben gets home, car still drive able, he leaves his daughter at home after the accident.

He gets to the party, starts work, and very slowly, the dull pain becomes very very unbearable. He finds it hard to concentrate on the most simple task. The pain was like 100 flyscreens, you weren't able to get a clear picture.

After Ben had finished work, he had alot to drink, but could hardly walk, his body had gone into shut down mode. He tried alcohol to get rid of the pain.

He was desperate, not thinking straight, he drove to the bridge between the 2 towns, and parked on the edge.

It was 60 to 80 feet high, Ben was crying as he was in pain bigtime. Just needed the pain to end.

He had 4 meters of chain, he padlocked one end to his car, then the other end around his neck. He then leaned on the edge of the bridge, in tears, he couldn't see any other way out of his pain.

30 minutes had gone by, and police cars and ambulances turned up. Blue and red lights flashing, it took an hour to convince Ben that he was not to do this to himself.

Ben did ask God in his need and prayed that God showed him he was loved.

God has impeccable timing!

The Grand Final.

*I*t's springtime, it has a distinctive fresh smell in the air, and slightly warmer. Football season is nearly over and just one last game, the grand final. It is an honor to be able play in one let alone win one.

Charlie had played in last year's grand final, but he was very sick with the flu. And they lost the grand final by 1 point. Charlie blamed himself for the loss because of being sick.

His grandfather had always said

"if you are able to walk, you can still bloody play footy " .

Charlie was sticking to these words from his grand father. He was always trying to impress his grandfather. His grand father was a life member of the club and had played in 7 premierships. A very well respected man in the club.

So it's no surprise that he was Charlie's hero, and loved his grandfather very very much.

The teams had done their final training runs, and teams are announced and pinned up on the main board in town for all to see.

Charlie was feeling confident this year, he is fit, fitter than last year and more hungry to win the premiership.

The key to playing in a premiership and winning one is to not change anything in your preparation or training. If you do, it's like rocking the boat and it upsets the apple cart.

Charlie sticks to his routines, bed at 10:30, breakfast of eggs on toast in the morning, get to the ground 2 hours before the game, hang out with team mates, watch the game till half time, then go in to get changed and ready to play.

Everyone is pumped, ready to combat the other team.

It's time!

The teams are both on the field, both have run through their team banners, and now both are lined up facing each other and the Australian national anthem is played.

The crows roar very loud after the anthem is finished. Both teams run out to the respective positions on the field. There is alot of tension between the two teams, in fact, all through the last 80 years, these two towns have hated each other.

Before the ball is even bounced there is a fight break out in the center square, looks to be the sign of things to come.

1st quarter is gone and Charlie's teamare 28 points in front. The other team seem to be only interested in playing the man not the ball.

2nd quarter ended with Charlie's team having a commanding lead of 65 points with 2 quarters left to play.

3rd quarter went by with no fight left in the other team, and when the final quarter was over, Charlie's team had won by 134 points.

The team were so happy and celebrated singing the club song, they then recieved their premiership medals and the big moment they all were playing for, all year they had been working together for the end result.

The Premiership Cup.

Where has your bayonet gone too?

*I*t's 8 weeks since the long arduous 13 week training course at 1RTB, (1st recruit training Battalion.

Kapooka is a great place to be either made or broken.

Jim has slowly but surely became one of the boys. He is getting along with everyone, one of his biggest fears is people not liking him.

In the past he has had difficulties with this, and has had major issues with being bullied. The Army can be a bit like that, if you are part of the group, or with the boys it makes things easier, but if your not part of the group, it can be painful.

So since being posted to Puckapunyal, young Jim has fitted in very well with everyone on the course. The course he is doing is the Cooks course in the catering corps.

The Cooks course goes for 6 months, it is a chefs course of 4 years cramed into 6 months. Technically when you become a Sargent then you are a qualified chef.

Jim also is playing Australian rules football for a team called The Rats Of Tabrook . He is having a very good season playing for the Rats, and he is very happy with life.

He is dating a young lady from a nice country town, and only just met before being based at Puckapunyal.

Dating for 3 months, and not even trying to do anything sexual. Jim believes in no sex before marriage, because he is a born again Christian. He just wants to treat her with the respect she deserves.

So it's 8 weeks since Kapooka, and Jim and his really close mate Tom have been told to do guard duty. Every night there are up to 16 soldiers doing guard duty. 2 hours on the front guard room and 2 hours walking around the grounds.

So you do 2 hours in the guard room, then 2 hours walking the grounds then rest for 4 hours. Sleep hopefully for 4 hours, but hard to do when doing guard duty, ends up being non stop shenanigans.

Tom and Jim finish their 2 hours on the gate, and put on their gear to do the 2 hours of walking the grounds.

45 minutes into the walk around, its 03:45hrs and they come across a large amount of kangaroo's grazing on the grass area.

Jim gets on the radio and reports them to the gate to let them know, as there was roughly 30 to 35 kangaroo's grazing. Jim still on the radio, starts telling the guards on the other radio, that there are 3 very very large kangaroo's coming towards them.

The fear in Jim's voice was humorous to Tom and the others on the other end of the radio. Jim grabbed his bayonet, the bayonet goes on the end of the SLR rifle.

The kangaroo's were 8 meters away now, and in a panic, Jim decides to throw his bayonet at the kangaroo's, and the bayonet stuck into the biggest kangaroo, and this angered the kangaroo.

It stood up and it had to be up to 7 foot tall. It was angry and made growling sounds, and started bounding towards Jim and Tom. Jim and Tom were in fits of laughter, and at the same time trying to run for dear life. Have you ever tried to run fast whilst laughing hysterical? It is near impossible.

They got to the laundry room, and waited out till the kangaroo's had gone back to the other kangaroo's.

They laughed and laughed as they walked back to the guard room.

The next day they had room inspection, and the Sargent doing the inspection is very very thorough.

"Where is your bayonet private G?" Screamed the Sargent.

Jim forgot about the bayonet,

"um," then Tom broke out in laughter, uncontrollable laughter, "it's in a kangaroo's chest last time we seen it" Jim slowly answered.

Discipline came Jim and Tom's way.

Jim had to pay $500 fine for losing his bayonet, and Tom had to do 200 push ups for laughing!

www.ingramcontent.com/pod-product-compliance
Lightning Source LLC
Chambersburg PA
CBHW040847120626
46547CB00001B/65